A Surprise in Disguise

Luke 24:13–35 for children

Written by Jeffrey E. Burkart • Illustrated by Michelle Dorenkamp

Arch® Books
Copyright © 1999 Concordia Publishing House
3558 S. Jefferson Avenue, St. Louis, MO 63118-3968
Printed in Colombia

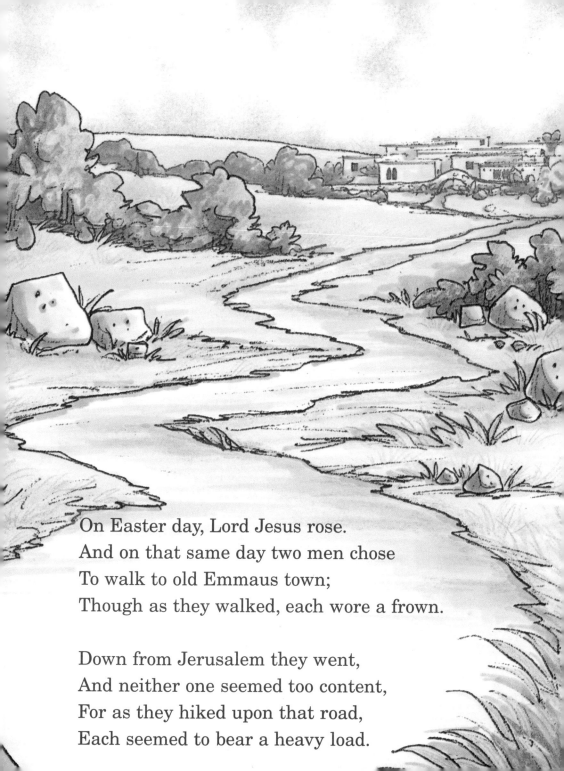

On Easter day, Lord Jesus rose.
And on that same day two men chose
To walk to old Emmaus town;
Though as they walked, each wore a frown.

Down from Jerusalem they went,
And neither one seemed too content,
For as they hiked upon that road,
Each seemed to bear a heavy load.

They talked about Lord Jesus' death.
They thought about His final breath.
And they remembered how He died—
How cruelly He'd been crucified!

Then on that path, to their surprise,
Lord Jesus walked, but in disguise.
They did not know He was the one
Who died and rose—God's only Son.

As Jesus joined them on their way,
He asked, "What's happening today?
What news from Zion have you heard?"
With downcast face, one said, "My word!

"Where have you been these past few days?
Have you been living in a haze?
The things that just have taken place
Are plain as this nose on my face!"

"What things?" He asked. "What do you mean?"
Then they replied, "The Nazarene,
Who was God's prophet, just was tried
And sentenced to be crucified.

"We all had hoped, before He fell,
That He'd redeem all Israel.
But it's been three days since He died,
Three days since He was crucified.

"And then, to our surprise today,
Some women we know came to say
That they had seen His empty tomb.
His body was not in that room.

"And then some angels came to say
That Jesus is alive today!
The women said, 'Those are the facts!'
Straight to that tomb some men made tracks.

"They ran as fast as they could go
To see if it was really so.
And when they peered into that place,
All that they found was empty space."

Then Jesus said, "You foolish guys!
How slow you are to realize
The truth of prophecies of old.
Do you not know what they foretold?

"They said that Christ would suffer death.
They said He'd spend His dying breath
Redeeming everyone from sin
So each a new life could begin!"

The three men walked into the town
Just as the sun was going down.
The two men pleaded, "Please, please stay
With us tonight. Don't go away!"

So Jesus stopped to have a bite
Of supper with those men that night.
And when He gave them bread to eat,
Their eyes were opened. What a treat!

The Savior vanished from their sight.
They said, "Did not our hearts ignite
Within us as He showed the way,
The truth, the life, to us today?"

Back to Jerusalem they sped.
They spread this news: "Christ is not dead!
Our Lord's alive, as live can be.
And we will live eternally!"

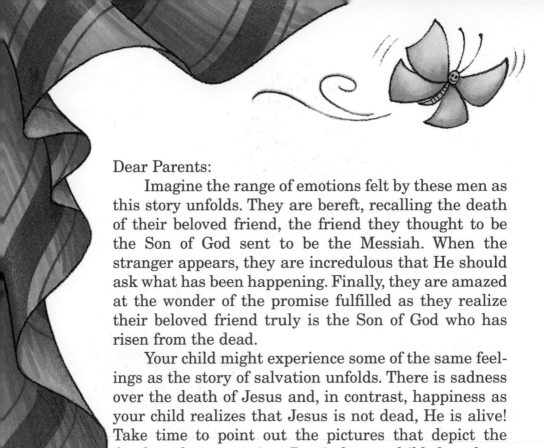

Dear Parents:

Imagine the range of emotions felt by these men as this story unfolds. They are bereft, recalling the death of their beloved friend, the friend they thought to be the Son of God sent to be the Messiah. When the stranger appears, they are incredulous that He should ask what has been happening. Finally, they are amazed at the wonder of the promise fulfilled as they realize their beloved friend truly is the Son of God who has risen from the dead.

Your child might experience some of the same feelings as the story of salvation unfolds. There is sadness over the death of Jesus and, in contrast, happiness as your child realizes that Jesus is not dead, He is alive! Take time to point out the pictures that depict the death and resurrection. Remind your child that these events were actually foretold years earlier.

Help your child see that the plan of salvation did not just happen; it was the fulfillment of a promise. The promise of salvation is for everyone. It is God's fervent desire that all people would come to faith, believing in the fulfillment of God's promise—a promise made for you and your child too.

The Editor